Searchlight BOOKS

How Does Government Work?

The Congress

A Look at the Legislative Branch

Robin Nelson and Sandy Donovan

Lerner Publications Company
Minneapolis

Lerner Publications Company
A division of Lerner Publishing Group, Inc.
241 First Avenue North
Minneapolis, MN 55401 U.S.A.

Website address: www.lernerbooks.com

Library of Congress Cataloging-in-Publication Data

Nelson, Robin, 1971–
     The Congress: a look at the legislative branch / by Robin Nelson and Sandy
Donovan.
          p.   cm. — (Searchlight books™—how does government work?)
     Includes index.
     ISBN 978-0-7613-6518-1 (lib. bdg. : alk. paper)
     1. United States. Congress—Juvenile literature. 2. Legislative power—United
States—Juvenile literature. 3. Legislation—United States—Juvenile literature.
4. Statutes—United States—Juvenile literature. I. Donovan, Sandra, 1967– II. Title.
III. Title: Making laws.
     JK1025.N45 2012
     328.73—dc22   2010042498

Manufactured in the United States of America
1 – DP – 12/31/11

Contents

Chapter 1

THE LEGISLATIVE BRANCH

In 1787, men from across the United States met and wrote the U.S. Constitution. The Constitution explains how the men thought the U.S. government should work.

George Washington (CENTER) heads the signing of the U.S. Constitution. What is explained in the U.S. Constitution?

The Constitution splits the government into three parts. The parts are called branches. The branches must work together.

The executive branch includes the president of the United States. It also includes those who work for the president. The judicial branch is the courts and judges. The legislative branch is Congress.

The U.S. Constitution defines the roles of each branch of government.

PRESIDENT BARACK OBAMA MAKES A SPEECH TO CONGRESS IN 2011.

The House and the Senate

Congress is made up of two groups of people. They are the House of Representatives (the House) and the Senate. Congress is in charge of making laws for the whole country.

The House has 435 members. The members are called representatives. They come from all fifty states. Each state has at least one representative. Big states have many representatives. Small states have few representatives.

Each state also has two senators. So there are one hundred senators in Congress.

Members of the House of Representatives raise their hands while they are sworn in. They are promising to support the Constitution.

Chapter 2

CONGRESS AND ITS JOBS

Congress's biggest job is to write, discuss, and pass, or approve, bills. A bill is a written plan for a new law. Bills are sent to the president to sign. If the president signs a bill, it becomes a law.

This bill is about health care. What is a bill?

Other Jobs

Members of Congress have other jobs too. They make laws that control trade between states and trade between America and other countries. They make laws about taxes and borrowing money. They approve the making of money. And they have the power to declare war.

Pictures of famous Americans are printed on U.S. money. Congress approves the making of money.

Chapter 3

LAWS, LAWS EVERYWHERE

Have you ever thought about the different kinds of laws our country has? Some laws tell us things we can't do, such as stealing. Other laws tell us things we have to do, such as going to school.

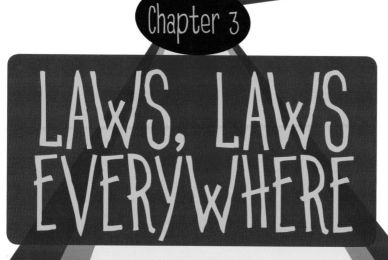

Kids have to go to school because it's the law. What different kinds of laws does our country have?

State and Federal Laws

Most laws are either state laws or federal laws. State governments make state laws. They apply only to that state.

THE SPEED LIMIT IS A STATE LAW.

Congress makes federal laws. They apply to the whole country.

President Lyndon B. Johnson signs the Civil Rights Act of 1964 into law. This federal law gives rights to Americans of all races.

Chapter 4

FROM IDEA TO BILL

Anyone can turn an idea into a law—even kids! When people think of an idea for a new law, they might try to get it made into a bill. Suppose you and your friends agree you don't want to go to school on Fridays. You already have your idea for a new law: no school on Fridays. The next step is to get that idea presented to Congress.

These students are researching an idea that might make a good law. What might people do if they think of an idea for a new law?

Presenting a Bill

Putting an idea in writing and presenting it to Congress makes it a bill. In this case, Representative Sue Smith decides to present the bill that would cancel school on Fridays. She is the bill's sponsor.

Representatives discuss a bill.

Sometimes when a sponsor presents a bill in the House, a similar bill is presented in the Senate. For a bill to become a law, both the House and the Senate must approve it. Having two bills makes this easier. That's because both the House and the Senate are discussing the same topic at the same time.

Senator Mitch McConnell speaks to other lawmakers in 2011.

In this case, Representative Smith talks with Senator Tom Moe. She wants him to sponsor a No School on Fridays bill in the Senate. Senator Moe agrees with most of Representative Smith's reasons for her bill. But he thinks there should be a few hours of school on Fridays. Senator Moe's bill is similar to Representative Smith's bill, except that it would cancel school only on Friday afternoons.

A senator (LEFT) talks with a representative (RIGHT) after a meeting. Senators and representatives sometimes discuss issues with one another.

Committees

In the Senate chamber (the Senate's main meeting room), Senator Moe stands up and presents his bill. Senate leaders decide to send the bill to a committee. Committees are small groups of senators or representatives. They discuss bills on certain topics. The committee will talk about the bill.

Representative Smith's bill has been sent to a House committee. Both committees will decide whether the rest of Congress should discuss the bill.

The Senate chamber, seen here in 1964, is where the Senate meets.

Time to Decide

Representative Smith tells the House committee why she thinks the bill is a good idea. She tells them canceling school on Fridays will be good for teachers and kids. She says it will save schools money.

Some people don't like this idea. Others ask more questions. The committee decides they like the bill. But they want to make one change. Instead of saying schools must close on Fridays, they want to say that schools have the choice of holding classes on Fridays or closing. They want each state to decide for itself. Representative Smith decides this is a good compromise (an agreement reached through each side giving up something).

A HOUSE COMMITTEE DISCUSSES A BILL.

HART

M. HOSTETTLER

After committee members have finished changing the bill, they decide whether they should recommend it to the whole House. All the representatives who like the bill raise their hands to vote. Representative Smith's bill passes.

This room is where the representatives vote.

The Senate committee has also approved Senator Moe's bill. The next step for his bill will be a discussion by the whole Senate.

THESE SENATORS TALK TO EACH OTHER ABOUT A BILL.

Chapter 5

DEBATING AND VOTING

The bill has its second reading in the House. This means it's read to all members present so they can suggest amendments, or changes.

This official reading of a bill in the House took place in 1914. What happens at a second reading in the House?

A representative raises his hand. He suggests a change to the bill. He wants to make sure that if schools save money by closing on Fridays, they will spend it on computers. He reads his amendment.

A few minutes later, the members vote on the amendment to make schools spend the money on computers. All those in favor say yea. All those against say nay. This is called a voice vote. Everyone can hear that there are more nays than yeas. The amendment doesn't pass.

This painting shows a voice vote in the House of Representatives in 1868.

Time for a House Vote

To vote on any bill, one-half of all the representatives must be present. An official sounds buzzers in the hallways and offices. The sound tells members it's time to go to the House chamber to vote. The members hurry to their seats. They press a button to be counted. With 240 buttons pressed, more than half of the 435 representatives are present. They can vote.

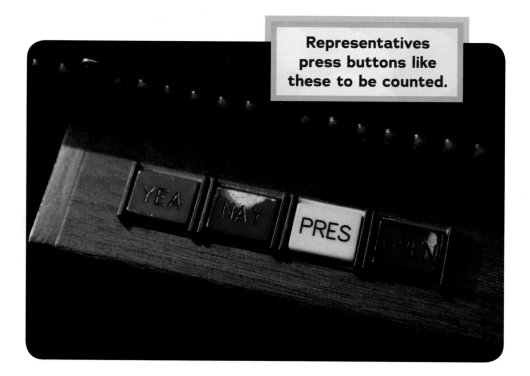

Representatives press buttons like these to be counted.

The bill has its third reading, and it's time to vote. The representatives say yea or nay. But it's hard to tell if there are more yeas or nays. To be sure, a standing vote is taken. This means all the representatives stand to be counted when they vote. A total of 130 representatives stand in favor of Representative Smith's bill. That's enough for the bill to pass.

This illustration shows the Speaker of the House of Representatives (the most senior House official) counting votes in 1873.

The Senate debates, or discusses, a bill in 1940.

Time for a Senate Vote

Senator Moe's bill comes up for a vote in the Senate. Representative Smith knows that if this bill does not pass the Senate, then her bill won't become a law.

In the Senate chamber, Senator Moe tells the other senators why he thinks his bill is a good idea. He tells them his bill would cancel school on Friday afternoons.

It's time to vote on the bill. An official calls out the senators' names. Most senators answer yea or nay. But two say present. They say this because they don't want to vote either yea or nay. When the official has called out all the names, the vote is counted: 47 yeas, 42 nays, and 2 presents. The bill has passed the Senate.

These senators are pictured in 2011. Each of them gets to vote on a bill when it's in the Senate.

Sorting Things Out

The House and the Senate have voted that schools can close on Fridays. But there's one problem. The bill approved in the House is different from the one approved in the Senate. Senators voted to cancel school on Friday afternoons. But in the House, representatives voted that schools should be able to make their own decisions about having classes on Fridays. Which bill should become a law?

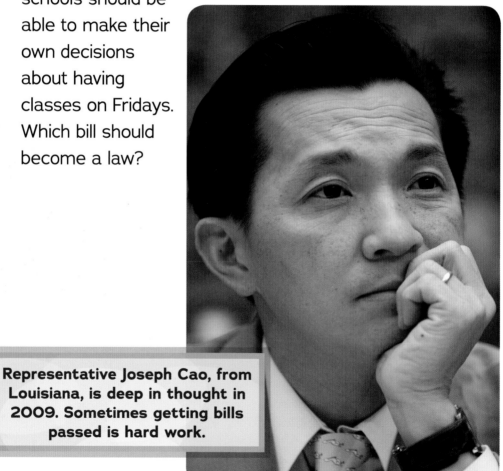

Representative Joseph Cao, from Louisiana, is deep in thought in 2009. Sometimes getting bills passed is hard work.

After much discussion, a conference committee agrees there's a better chance the president would sign the House bill. (A conference committee is a group of senators and representatives who talk about what to do when different bills are passed in the House and the Senate.) After all, the House bill gives states the choice to close school on Fridays. The Senate bill would make all schools close on Friday afternoons.

This cartoon shows a member of Congress pushing a favorite bill through committee while another bill is left behind. Sometimes congresspeople favor certain bills over others.

Chapter 6

GETTING SIGNED INTO LAW

The president's desk is the final stop for a bill. The president has three choices when bills are presented: sign, veto, or do nothing. If the president agrees with the bill, the president can sign it. Then it becomes law. If the president disagrees with the bill, the next step is to veto it. That means the bill is rejected. The bill will not become a law unless Congress votes to override, or cancel, the veto. To override the veto, two-thirds of the members of both the House and the Senate have to pass the bill again.

Bills are delivered to the Oval Office for the president to review. What three choices does the president have when bills are presented?

The president has ten days to either sign or veto the bill. If the president doesn't do anything, then the bill becomes law.

President George W. Bush signs a bill to provide hurricane relief in 2005.

Signing Ceremonies

When the president signs bills into law, a signing ceremony sometimes takes place. The president uses several pens to sign the bill. Then the president hands the pens to the bill's sponsors and to other people to whom the new law is important.

President Barack Obama chooses one of many pens to sign a bill into law at a signing ceremony.

Other times, the president doesn't have a ceremony. The bills are signed and sent back to Congress. Usually the president does this with less important bills.

The Buck Stops Here sign sits on President Harry S. Truman's desk. The sign means that Truman felt he had the final say about bills and other matters related to running the country.

Making a Decision

The president has a tough decision to make. He would like to sign the bill into law because he's a friend of Representative Smith and Senator Moe. But he doesn't agree with them. He thinks education is very important. He believes school should be held on Fridays. He thinks kids need as much schooling as they can get.

These students learn in school. Do you think school should be held on Fridays?

The president wants to veto the bill. But he needs to make sure he has all his facts straight. His staff has prepared a report listing the reasons people supported or rejected the bill when it was before Congress.

The president stays up until two in the morning reading through this report. He thinks there are good arguments from both sides. But he hasn't changed his mind. He is going to veto the bill.

President Jimmy Carter reads over documents in his office in 1979.

35

The Final Decision

The next day, the president writes a veto message to Congress. This message officially vetoes the bill and explains the reasons behind the veto. The president sends the bill and the message to Congress.

President Ulysses S. Grant writes a veto message to Congress to explain why he vetoed a bill.

Representative Smith and Senator Moe don't think they can get enough votes to override the veto. But when Congress meets again next year, Representative Smith and Senator Moe may try again. The bills could go through all the steps of becoming a law again.

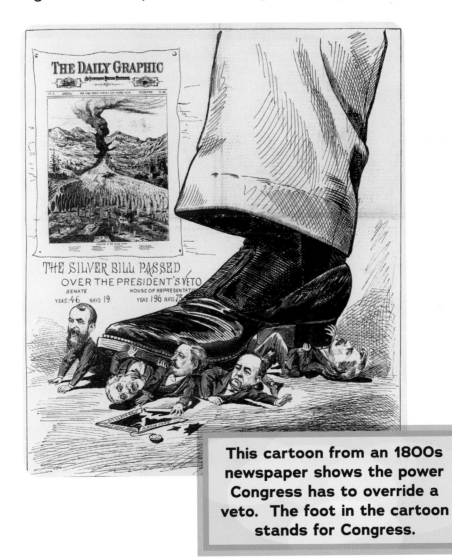

This cartoon from an 1800s newspaper shows the power Congress has to override a veto. The foot in the cartoon stands for Congress.

Glossary

amendment: a change that is made to a bill or a law

bill: a written plan for a new law

committee: a small group of senators or representatives. Committees discuss bills on certain topics.

compromise: an agreement that is reached by opposing sides giving up some of their demands

conference committee: a group of senators and representatives who discuss what to do when different bills are passed in the House and the Senate

Congress: a group of elected officials who write, debate, and make laws. Congress is made up of the Senate and the House of Representatives.

executive branch: the branch of government that is led by the president. The executive branch enforces laws of the United States.

judicial branch: the branch of government involving the court system

legislative branch: the branch of government that makes laws

override: to cancel a veto

sponsor: the person who presents a bill to Congress

tax: money that people and businesses must pay to support a government

veto: to reject a bill

Learn More about Government

Books

Gorman, Jacqueline Laks. *Why Do We Have Laws?* Pleasantville, NY: Weekly Reader Books, 2008. Gorman explores laws and why we have them.

Kowalski, Kathiann M. *Judges and Courts: A Look at the Judicial Branch*. Minneapolis: Lerner Publications Company, 2012. Find out about the judicial branch and its role in government.

Landau, Elaine. *The President, Vice President, and Cabinet: A Look at the Executive Branch*. Minneapolis: Lerner Publications Company, 2012. Learn how the executive branch contributes to our government.

Taylor-Butler, Christine. *The Congress of the United States*. New York: Children's Press, 2008. Read more about Congress and what it does.

Websites

Ben's Guide to U.S. Government for Kids
http://bensguide.gpo.gov/3-5/index.html
This website includes lots of useful information about the U.S. government.

Congress for Kids
http://www.congressforkids.net
Read up on Congress at this fun site.

Kids in the House
http://kids.clerk.house.gov
Check out this interesting page from the Office of the Clerk of the U.S. House of Representatives.

Index

Photo Acknowledgments

The images in this book are used with the permission of: Library of Congress LC-USZC4-2541, p. 4; National Archives, p. 5; © Brendan Smialowski/Getty Images, p. 6; AP Photo/Susan Walsh, p. 7; © Scott J. Ferrell/Congressional Quarterly/Getty Images, pp. 8, 14, 19, 21, 27; © Brie Cohen/Independent Picture Service, p. 9; © Comstock Images, p. 10; © Rob Byron/Shutterstock.com, p. 11; Lyndon Baines Johnson Library and Museum, p. 12; © Andersen Ross/Photodisc/Getty Images, p. 13; REUTERS/Ho New, p. 15; © Mannie Garcia/Bloomberg/Getty Images, p. 16; © Roddey Mims/Bettmann/CORBIS, p. 17; © Tim Sloan/AFP/Getty Images, p. 18; © Owen Franken/CORBIS, p. 20; © Bettmann/CORBIS, pp. 22, 26; © CORBIS, pp. 23, 35, 36, 37; © Brendan Hoffman/Getty Images, p. 24; © Kean Collection/Archive Photos/Getty Images, p. 25; © Andrew Harrer/Bloomberg/Getty Images, p. 28; The Granger Collection, NYC — All rights reserved, p. 29; © Jewel Samad/AFP/Getty Images, p. 30; © Paul Morse/The White House via Getty Images, p. 31; © Alex Wong/Getty Images, p. 32; Harry S. Truman Library, p. 33; © Ryan McVay/Taxi/Getty Images, p. 34.

Front cover: © Joshua Roberts/Bloomberg/Getty Images.

Main body text set in Adrianna Regular 14/20
Typeface provided by Chank